Marty Stouffer's Wild Animal Babies

From the PBS Television Series WILD AMERICA

Text adapted by Rita Walsh • Illustrated by Turi MacCombie

A GOLDEN BOOK • NEW YORK
Western Publishing Company, Inc., Racine, Wisconsin 53404

© 1990 Marty Stouffer. Illustrations © 1990 Turi MacCombie. All rights reserved. Printed in the U.S.A. No part of this book may be reproduced or copied in any form without written permission from the publisher. GOLDEN, GOLDEN & DESIGN, GOLDENCRAFT, A GOLDEN BOOK, and A GOLDEN LOOK-LOOK BOOK are registered trademarks of Western Publishing Company, Inc. Library of Congress Catalog Card Number: 89-51824 ISBN: 0-307-12576-9/ISBN: 0-307-62576-1 (lib. bdg.)   ABCDEFGHIJKLM

Everyone loves babies. There's something very special about them. Maybe it's the way they look at the world with their wide, bright eyes, or the way they struggle to stand for the very first time. Perhaps it's the way they play, turning life into a rough-and-tumble adventure.

As babies play they learn more and more about the world around them. This is true for animal babies as well as human babies. Playing helps babies grow up.

Raccoon babies are called kits. Even while they are young, kits are *very* curious about the world around them. They have front paws like human hands, and they like to pick up and examine all kinds of things they find in the forest.

Raccoons learn by doing the same things they see their mother doing. As they become good climbers, they learn to find food in trees. As they become good swimmers, they can catch frogs and crayfish in streams. By the time they have grown up, kits have learned all they need to know to live on their own in the wild.

Baby deer are called fawns. They grow up in the forest, too. The things they have to learn are different from what raccoons learn.

Fawns are born in the springtime. Sometimes a mother deer has twin fawns. The fawns have long, graceful legs and can stand up right away. Their long legs help them to run very fast if danger is near.

Fawns must learn to be careful and use their senses to detect enemies. They learn to lie very still in the forest—so still that their spotted backs look the same as the ground around them. If a mountain lion comes by, it won't even see the little fawns hiding.

Bear cubs don't have to worry about hiding. Their mothers are able to protect them, so they aren't afraid of other animals. Cubs may seem to be very roly-poly and carefree, but they are learning new things all the time.

Cubs love to play. They chase each other up and down trees and into hollow logs. They like to splash in streams. They wrestle and run. All this exercise makes them very strong. Soon they are able to catch their own fish for dinner and protect their own cubs. But even when they are grown up, bears still like to play.

Cougar babies are also called cubs. Cougar cubs look like cuddly kittens. After they are born, their mother hides them in a cave and goes out to hunt for fresh meat. While she is out the cubs play with each other. They pounce on each other from rocks inside the cave. They snarl and hiss. They pretend that they are hunting, too.

When they get bigger, their mother will teach them how to hunt. The cubs will learn to hide in trees. When they are on their own, they will catch food for themselves. It takes a long time for cougar cubs to learn these things.

Lynx babies look like funny kittens! They have very big feet and short, stubby tails. Their ears have pointy tufts of fur at the tips. Their fur is very thick and keeps them warm during cold, harsh winters. When they walk on the snow, their big feet keep them from sinking into it.

Lynx babies stay with their mother for a whole year. They even follow her when she hunts. Their mother's strong legs help her run very fast, fast enough to catch a snowshoe hare for her babies to eat.

Wolf puppies don't live with just their mother and father. They live in a pack. All the adult wolves in the pack help to take care of the puppies, just like baby-sitters who watch children whose parents are away.

Wolf puppies play all the time. They love to play with bones left over from their dinner. They bite on the bones and snarl if other puppies try to steal them. They play with each other and the adult members of the pack. This is how they make friends. When they are grown up, all the wolves hunt together, and share their food with new puppies.

Baby owls are called owlets. Owlets don't play very much. They are too busy eating! Owlets eat nearly all the time. Both parents take care of the baby owls. They take turns catching food for their tiny, fluffy babies. Owls like to eat mice. They have to fly very fast to catch them.

Owlets grow up in cozy nests that their parents have built for them. Their wings become covered with feathers and get stronger every day. When they are ready to fly, the baby owls are called fledglings. Fledglings must practice flying for a few weeks before they are fast enough to catch mice all by themselves. Even after they learn to fly, the fledglings' parents continue to bring them food. Owls take good care of their young.

    Bunnies are born in a nest very similar to the owls' nest. But their nests are hidden underground. Mother rabbits are called does, and they make the nest soft by lining it with fur pulled from their own bellies. It's important for the nest to be soft and warm because baby rabbits are born without any fur. They also can't see or hear for about ten days. The tiny bunnies grow up warm and safe in their dark underground nest.

After about two weeks the bunnies are big enough to go outside. Now they must learn about the outside world. Bunnies don't have sharp claws or teeth to protect themselves, so they learn to run in a zig-zag pattern to confuse and tire the animals that hunt them.

Skunk babies are called kits—the same as raccoon babies. Skunk kits eat berries, insects, small lizards, and snakes. By following their mother everywhere, the skunk kits learn the best places to find food.

Baby skunks have a very unusual way of protecting themselves. When they are frightened, they just lift their striped tails and spray a bad-smelling scent at whatever is bothering them. The other forest animals usually leave the skunk family alone!

Porcupine babies also have a unique way of defending themselves. They are born with soft quills covering their bodies. The quills have sharp tips that become hard soon after the porcupine babies are born. With their pointy suits of armor, baby porcupines have no reason to fear any other forest animals.

Young porcupines also learn by copying their mother. They do not play much. A mother porcupine and her babies walk great distances looking for tasty, crisp plants, berries, shrubs, and tree bark to eat. For young porcupines, growing up in the forest is sometimes hard work!

Animal babies grow up much faster than boys and girls. They become adults after only a few short months. However, their play serves an important purpose—teaching the animal babies the skills they need to survive. When these animals have babies of their own, the babies play the same way their parents once did, and learn all the important lessons they need to grow up in the wild.

New

f9 293

New Virginia Public Library
30000816

```
E                               92
Walsh, Rita
Wild Animal Babies
```

DATE DUE			
DEC 21 1993			
SEP 05 1995			
MY 11 02			
AP 03			
AUG 29 2007			
NOV 21 2012			
OCT 16 2013			
AUG 22 2017			

NEW VIRGINIA PUBLIC LIBRARY
408 West St.
P.O. Box 304
NEW VIRGINIA, IA 50210-0304